REVISION NOTES FOR ORDINARY LEVEL ECONOMIC AND SOCIAL HISTORY (FROM 1760)

REVISION NOTES FOR ORDINARY LEVEL

ECONOMIC AND SOCIAL HISTORY

(FROM 1760)

By

F. M. BATTY, B.A.

ALLMAN & SON (Publishers) LTD

17–19 FOLEY STREET, LONDON W1A 1DR

First published 1966

Reprinted (revised) 1969
Reprinted 1971
Reprinted (revised) 1974
Reprinted 1976 & 1980

ISBN 0.204.74682.5

Made and printed in Great Britain by
Butler & Tanner Ltd, Frome and London

CONTENTS

1

AGRICULTURE

Open Field System

Introduced by Saxons—replaced enclosed field system of Celts. Not found in all parts of England, *e.g.*, not in West of England. Still in use in most of England in 1700.

Three main parts:

1. FIELDS

(*a*) Three in number.
(*b*) Divided into strips—about one acre each.
(*c*) One field fallow each year:

Year	*Field A*	*Field B*	*Field C*
1st	Wheat	Fallow	Barley
2nd	Barley	Wheat	Fallow
3rd	Fallow	Barley	Wheat
4th	Rotation starts again		

(*d*) Each farmer had strips scattered over each field.
(*e*) No hedges divided the strips or fields—baulks or posts used.

2. MEADOW

(*a*) Each farmer entitled to harvest hay.
(*b*) Otherwise land open for grazing after hay harvest.

3. COMMON

All landowners could:

(*a*) Pasture animals.
(*b*) Collect fuel.
(*c*) Collect berries.

Cottagers and 'squatters' used commons but had no legal right.

Criticism of Open Field System

1. AGRICULTURE

(*a*) Inadequate winter feeding stuffs cut down number of animals.
(*b*) Thus amount of manure limited.
(*c*) Continual growth of cereals exhausted the soil.
(*d*) Third or more of land wasted in fallow every year.

2. STRIP SYSTEM

(*a*) Difficulty of access.
(*b*) Arguments and dishonesty over boundaries and crop stealing.
(*c*) Time wasted in moving from strip to strip.
(*d*) Spread of weeds—no hedges to hold them back, and one bad strip could infect others because close together.
(*e*) Damage from straying cattle.
(*f*) Impracticable for individual to improve drainage.
(*g*) Farmer could not grow a crop different to that of his neighbour, if sowing or reaping time different, because cattle turned out onto fields after harvest.

3. COMMON LAND

(*a*) Much waste, poor pasture.
(*b*) Difficult to prevent overstocking.
(*c*) Diseases spread easily.
(*d*) Selective breeding difficult.

4. METHOD OF CULTIVATION

(*a*) Ploughing—heavy wooden plough—needed six to eight oxen, two men and a boy.
(*b*) Sowing—broadcast system—much waste and uneven spreading.
(*c*) Weeding not possible as plants not in rows.
(*d*) Reaping—hand scythes and sickles.
(*e*) Threshing—flail used.

Improvement difficult

Because:

(*a*) Productivity adequate to supply the small population of early 18th century, therefore no very great demand for increased production.
(*b*) Poor transport limited markets and prevented spread of new ideas.
(*c*) Farmers, being tenants, were liable to eviction at short notice.

(*d*) Lack of capital among small farmers who were often illiterate, ignorant and conservative.
(*e*) Cottagers often lived at low level on produce of common, and therefore there was some reluctance to deprive them of the use of that land.

Enclosures

Why?

(*a*) Increase of population—far more food needed.
(*b*) Wars of 1793 to 1815 meant less food imports.
(*c*) Improved methods (see below) could not be introduced under Open Field System.
(*d*) Wider markets as transport improved.

How?

(*a*) Private acts of Parliament. First general act passed in 1801.
(*b*) Land surveyed.
(*c*) All land, including common and meadow, re-distributed.
(*d*) Common rights to land abolished as land enclosed.
(*e*) New fields separated by hedges and fences.

Results

Economically good but, at least in the short run, socially bad.

1. ECONOMIC RESULTS

(*a*) Greater efficiency—more yield per acre.
(*b*) More farm land available.
(*c*) Greater food output.
(*d*) New methods introduced (see below).

2. SOCIAL RESULTS

(*a*) Problem of landless labourer.
(*b*) Smallholder could not compete with large farmer.
(*c*) Cost of fencing not always met.
(*d*) Loss of common land and decline of domestic industry led to poverty.
(*e*) Fewer labourers needed due to new methods.
(*f*) Large-scale move to new industrial towns.
(*g*) Steady collapse of Poor Law (see p. 43).
(*h*) 'Squatters' lost their land on common unless they had held it for twenty years.

Between the years 1760 and 1797 about 1,500 Enclosure Acts were passed. By 1810 the number had reached 3,554.

Pioneers of English Agriculture

Jethro Tull (1674–1741)

Experiments:

(*a*) Grew turnips, sainfoin and potatoes.
(*b*) Selected seeds.
(*c*) Invented seed drill which sowed seeds evenly and in lines.
(*d*) As seed sown in lines horse hoe could be used.

In 1733 published results in book, *Horse Hoeing Husbandry*. Criticised nowadays because:

(*a*) Rotation of crops not advocated.
(*b*) Manuring not recommended.
(*c*) His methods pulverised the soil.

Viscount Townshend (1674–1738)

Improvements:

(*a*) Enclosed his land.
(*b*) Added marl (clay and lime) to sandy surface soil.
(*c*) Used Tull's methods.
(*d*) Introduced Norfolk Four Course Rotation (turnips and clover as new crops. Clover replenishes the soil with nitrogen and because of this a year in which the land lay fallow was no longer necessary. Turnips enabled the farmers to keep livestock through the winter, by providing fodder.)

Robert Bakewell (1725–1795)

Concentrated on stock-breeding:

(*a*) Had enclosed farm of 440 acres—land laid down mostly for grass; rest for fodder crops.
(*b*) Animals well-housed, well-fed and clean.
(*c*) Bred animals for meat.
(*d*) Bred New Leicester sheep, for meat and not only for wool as previously.

Arthur Young (1741–1820)

The publiciser of the Agricultural Revolution:

(*a*) Farmer—carried out 3,000 experiments.
(*b*) Wrote about old methods of farming and suggested improvements.
(*c*) Went on lecture tours—wrote books on them, *e.g.*, *Six Weeks' Tour in the Southern Counties of England and Wales*.
(*d*) 1793—Secretary of the Board of Agriculture.

Depression (1830–1850)

Why?

(*a*) Speculation—farmers had not recovered from bad effects of speculation during and after French Wars.
(*b*) Poor Law—wages fell to starvation level, poor rate rose, and farmers were ruined and labourers demoralised. Poor Law Amendment Act left low wages and fear of workhouse.
(*c*) General Depression—felt in trade and industry—meant there was no market for agricultural products.
(*d*) Corn Laws—no incentive to grow.

Golden Age of English Agriculture (1850–1875)

Why?

(*a*) More education of farmers—foundation of agricultural colleges.
(*b*) Agricultural science developed—artificial fertilisers (phosphates, potash, nitrates, etc.).
(*c*) Drainage with clay pipes. Experiments by Laws.
(*d*) Increased use of machinery, *e.g.*, steam pumps for drainage, haymaking machines, etc.
(*e*) Railways—cattle and perishable foodstuffs travelled more easily and more quickly by rail to wider markets.
(*f*) Increased efficiency—less labour and lower wage costs.
(*g*) Great expansion of demand with rise in population and standard of living.
(*h*) Low agricultural wages.

Benefits

(*a*) Old-fashioned and poor farms go.
(*b*) Small farms amalgamated into larger ones.
(*c*) Healthy cattle, good crops, marshes drained.
(*d*) Most English food was English grown.

Depression in English Agriculture (1875–1899)

As in industry:

(*a*) Loss of purchasing power.
(*b*) Falling profits.
(*c*) General depression.

Accentuated by bad harvests of 1873, 1875, 1876 and 1879.

Results

(*a*) Prices fell.
(*b*) Profits and rents fell.
(*c*) Farms unlet.
(*d*) Average quantity of wheat per acre fell.
(*e*) Agricultural capital diminished.
(*f*) Land under cultivation grew less.
(*g*) Foreign imports increased.

Why?

(*a*) Opening-up of prairies of N. America resulted in an influx of cheap wheat to Britain; wheat prices were reduced by up to 60%.
(*b*) Import of cheap frozen or chilled meat.
(*c*) Later, New Zealand, Australia and Argentina sent dairy produce, meat, fertiliser and fodder.
(*d*) Royal Commission of 1882 blamed the following:
   (*i*) Weather—most important in their eyes.
   (*ii*) Imported food.
   (*iii*) High rents.
   (*iv*) Lack of capital.
   (*v*) No compensation to tenants for improvements made.
   (*vi*) Low wages.
(*e*) Commission of 1893 blamed foreign competition.

Remedies Advocated

(*a*) Increase in dairy farming.
(*b*) Breeding of pedigree stock.
(*c*) Market gardening developed—there was a growing home market for produce as industrial towns expanded and transport improved.
(*d*) Government help:
   (*i*) Rate reduction for farmers.
   (*ii*) Agricultural Holdings Act—some compensation for improvements.
   (*iii*) Ministry of Agriculture set up.

20th-Century Agriculture

1900–1914

Some slight improvement with the introduction of more diversity.

(*a*) Other forms of produce, *e.g.*, fruit and vegetables.
(*b*) Still pedigree stock-breeding.
(*c*) Dairy farming, but still faced by foreign competition.
(*d*) Small holdings, but not very effective because holders often

inexperienced and *renting* of such holdings was found not to encourage improvements.

1914–1919 Prosperity due largely to:

(*a*) Price control.
(*b*) Subsidies.
(*c*) State control.
(*d*) Arable land restored—more cereals grown.

1920–1939 General Depression because:

(*a*) Subsidies and State help stopped.
(*b*) Growing foreign competition.
(*c*) Free trade abandoned. Colonial preference took its place.
(*d*) Low prices.
(*e*) Demand for dairy produce increased.
(*f*) People continued to leave country areas.

1939–1945 WAR

(*a*) *County War Agricultural Committees:*
 (*i*) Farmers directed as to crops grown.
 (*ii*) Inefficient farmers removed.
 (*iii*) Grass lands ploughed.
 (*iv*) Machinery and fertilisers provided.
(*b*) ***Agricultural Research Council*** set up.
(*c*) ***Agricultural Improvement Council*** (*1941*)—to help to apply research to practical farming.
(*d*) Wheat rose in price.
(*e*) Excellent harvests.
(*f*) Labour problems largely solved by directed labour.

Post-1945

(*a*) County Agricultural Committees replace wartime committees.
(*b*) Hill Farming Acts (1946 and 1956) gave government grants for the rehabilitation of land.
(*c*) Marketing Boards
 1954 Potato Board
 1957 Egg M.B. and Pig Industry Development Board
 N.B. The Milk Marketing Board had been established in 1931.
(*d*) The growth of voluntary Co-operative Associations of farmers to facilitate sale and marketing of produce.
(*e*) Increased mechanisation leading to less use of manual labour.
(*f*) Agriculture and Horticulture Act (1964) gave government power to introduce minimum agricultural import prices.

1973—Entry to the *Common Market* (see p. 26).

2

INDUSTRY

Domestic Industry

Woollen Industry

This was the main industry in three areas:

1. East Anglia.
2. South West.
3. West Riding.

In 1 and 2 industry was controlled by capitalist clothiers who often supplied raw materials, rented out machinery and also marketed the finished product made in homes. In 3 it was usual to find the early master clothiers employing men in small workshops.

Requirements of Woollen Industry

(*a*) Raw wool.
(*b*) Fuel.
(*c*) Soft water—cleaning and dyeing.
(*d*) Water power—fulling.
(*e*) Fuller's earth.

The important factor was a good supply of water and the South West, with its capitalist system, developed this and the other resources best.

Processes

(*a*) Washing.
(*b*) Carding and combing—fibres separated ready for spinning.
(*c*) Spinning—thread made.
(*d*) Weaving—thread made up into cloth on a loom.
(*e*) Finishing—such processes as fulling (cleansing and thickening), dyeing and bleaching.

1. EAST ANGLIAN WOOLLEN INDUSTRY

Organised by clothiers who bought the wool of the Lincoln and Leicester breeds of sheep.

Norfolk

Specialised in worsteds (especially round Norwich) and light fabrics of worsted type. These required no fulling—there was no water power here.

Suffolk and Essex

Originally produced broadcloth but later spun wool for worsted weavers of Norfolk. Colchester noted for baize.

2. SOUTH-WEST WOOLLEN INDUSTRY

Clothiers responsible for organising manufacture at all stages.

Exeter specialised in serge and held a weekly market, but much cloth was sent to London to be sold. Some yarn imported from Ireland and Spain, via Bideford and Barnstaple.

3. WEST RIDING WOOLLEN INDUSTRY

Not controlled by wealthy clothiers but by small clothiers who owned their own looms and sold sufficient to buy next week's supply of wool. Some clothiers employed others in their workshops.

At end of the 17th century they started to produce fine woollens. Industry centred round Halifax, Huddersfield, Bradford, Leeds and Wakefield, with cloth halls at Halifax, Leeds and Wakefield to market the cloth.

Advantages of Domestic System

(*a*) It could be carried on in country districts where cost of living lower and living conditions healthier.

(*b*) A worker could work when, where and how he liked and could work for different clothiers and have alternative occupations, *e.g.*, farming.

(*c*) Tax collectors and the competitors of the clothier could not find out the state of his business and, if trade was slack, production could be stopped at no cost to himself.

Disadvantages of the Domestic System

(*a*) Lack of supervision led to stealing of materials, skimped work and delays.

(*b*) Workers were often in debt to employers or moneylenders for materials, advances on wages, money paid when sick or out of work and for tools or rent of tools.

(*c*) Due to the dispersed nature of industry workers had no bargaining power which led to unfair pay deductions, poor materials, payment in truck, etc.

(*d*) Work was irregular and this led to idleness followed by excessive bursts of work which in their turn led to great strain on a man and his wife and children.
(*e*) Home cluttered up with tools, work, etc.
(*f*) Clothier and workers were worlds apart and often disliked each other—thus it was difficult to introduce new methods and the West Riding was given an advantage because clothiers there were small, self-employed masters.

The Industrial Revolution

Period 1760–1830 known as the 'Industrial Revolution', but changes which took place cannot be restricted to this period alone.

1. Cotton

SLOW GROWTH UP TO 1760

(*a*) A new commodity for which a taste grew only slowly.
(*b*) Parliament passed laws in 1700 and 1720 forbidding the import and the wearing of printed cotton cloth (repealed in 1775).
(*c*) General shortage of labour—in competition with existing textile industries.
(*d*) Raw material had to be imported, mainly from Levant and West Indies.

RAPID GROWTH AFTER 1760

(*a*) Invention and use of machinery overcame shortage of labour and cut down production costs.
(*b*) Development of cotton-growing in southern U.S.A.
(*c*) Large potential demand for cheap washable clothing.
(*d*) Britain had wide overseas trade connections and an assured access to foreign markets where population was growing.
(*e*) Britain's two main competitors were weak:

(*i*) France held back by revolution and war.
(*ii*) India controlled by Britain.

Early Adoption of Machinery

(*a*) Reasons given above.
(*b*) Cotton fibres suitable for machinery as they are smooth, strong and inelastic (*cf.*, wool fibres).
(*c*) As it was a new industry there was a shortage of labour and

machines could take place of labour more easily than in older industries.

(*d*) Less bound by Government regulations and tradition.

Concentration of Cotton Industry in Lancashire

(*a*) Relative shortage of alternative work—agriculture poor—although there was a textile tradition.
(*b*) Liverpool had wide trading connections especially with West Indies and southern states of U.S.A.
(*c*) Natural resources:
   (*i*) Pennine streams—for power.
   (*ii*) Lancashire coalfield.
   (*iii*) Soft water.
   (*iv*) Damp atmosphere—prevents threads snapping.

New Machinery

Prior to Industrial Revolution processes carried out as follows:

(*a*) Spinning—with distaff and spindle or spinning wheel.
(*b*) Weaving—hand loom.

1733—Flying Shuttle—invented by *Kay*—shuttle mounted on wheels and jerked across loom by means of a spring.

Effects:

(*a*) Cloth could be wider—hitherto cloth only as wide as weaver could throw shuttle.
(*b*) Looms worked so quickly that there was insufficient yarn.

1764—Spinning Jenny—invented by *Hargreaves*—long wooden frame with single wheel which worked eight distaffs and spindles. By 1788 it was turning eighty spindles and needed special workshops, thus threatening the home spinners.

Thread produced was not strong enough for warp and was only used for weft.

1769—Water Frame—invented by *Arkwright* but based on work of Paul and Wyatt. Rollers used to draw out thread and the power used was water. Produced coarse strong yarn suitable for warp. Too large for use in home so Arkwright built mills to house new machinery. Arkwright often called 'Father of the Factory System'.

1779—Mule—invented by *Crompton.* Combined principles of water frame and jenny—produced fine strong yarn.

1785—Power Loom—invented by *Cartwright.* Rather clumsy at first.

Steam-driven after 1789 and in more general use, in an improved form, after 1830.

With this new machinery came the FACTORY SYSTEM with industry now concentrated in large towns on or near coalfields.

2. Wool

Changes came more slowly:

(*a*) Early inventions did not apply so easily to wool—snapped when spun on early jennies and mules.
(*b*) News of inventions travelled slowly—industry dispersed.
(*c*) Small woollen workers and bigger master clothiers were slow to adopt new machinery—they had been regulated so long by Parliament they could not see changes coming.

1. SOUTH-WEST ENGLAND

Jenny not used till 1790. Flying Shuttle not used in Wiltshire until 1800, and in Somerset till 1822. Mule did not appear until 1825.

2. EAST ANGLIA

None of the new inventions appeared at all and the industry gradually died out.

3. WEST RIDING

Spinning Jenny used first in 1780. But as late as 1806 Domestic System still in operation—many small masters employing two to ten workers.

In 1809 the laws restricting the number of machines in workshops were repealed. In 1798 the first spinning mills run by steam appeared in Bradford. In 1826 the first power loom came into use but home industry lingered on for quite a while after that.

Why Woollen Industry Settled in West Riding

(*a*) Soft water from Pennine streams.
(*b*) Power from Pennine streams.
(*c*) Local supplies of coal important when steam engine came into use.
(*d*) Close to Lancashire, home of the new inventions.
(*e*) Lack of tradition and old-established methods, therefore new inventions adopted more readily.
(*f*) Iron industry to supply new machinery.
(*g*) Over-confidence of older areas with a tradition of doing well.

(*h*) Older areas often made fancy cloths, especially East Anglia, which did not have such a wide market.
(*j*) Masters in older areas fond of a luxurious life and unwilling to accept hardships of new industrial era.

3. Iron

Two main processes:

(*a*) Production of pig iron from iron ore using a furnace.
(*b*) From this, cast iron and wrought iron are made. (Later, steel was manufactured also.)

Iron has been manufactured in this country since Roman times and the industry flourished in the Middle Ages. The industry was usually found in forested areas because of the use of charcoal as a fuel:

(*a*) Weald of Kent and Sussex.
(*b*) Forest of Dean.
(*c*) Wrekin District of Shropshire.

Timber was needed for ship construction and an act of Elizabeth I restricted the use of certain wood to ship-building.

By 1740 the annual production of iron was less than 18,000 tons and iron was imported from Sweden, Russia and the American colonies. A new fuel was needed—COAL. This was unsuitable at first as the fumes made the iron too brittle.

DUD DUDLEY

He experimented in smelting with coal about 1621. It is not known if he succeeded as the results of his experiments died with him.

ABRAHAM DARBY I (1677–1717)

He originally lived in Bristol. Moved to Coalbrookdale (Shropshire). First succeeded in smelting iron with coke in 1709. Kept the method within the family.

ABRAHAM DARBY II (1711–1765)

He carried on his father's work and improved on the blast in his furnace. BUT the iron produced by their methods was unsuitable for the production of wrought iron.

HENRY CORT (1740–1800)

The problem of Darby's furnace was solved in 1784 when Cort patented the Puddling Furnace, which drove a hot flame over bars of molten pig-iron which were then stirred to remove impurities. The iron produced could then be used for wrought iron. He also invented a rolling mill which took the place of hammering and helped remove impurities. The iron produced was much more malleable and cheaper than previously.

Two other improvements aided the iron industry:

1828—Nielson's Hot Blast—much fuel saved by heating the blast on the furnace and inferior coal could be used.
1839—Nasmyth's Steam Hammer—instead of hammering huge pieces of metal on a forge they were fed into a guillotine-like hammer.

Iron was popularised by the great iron-masters notably *John Wilkinson*, 1728–1808 (see p. 18).

4. Steam Engine

Water was the first form of power used in the Industrial Revolution apart from manual labour and the use of animals. It was unreliable and led to the scattering of industry along the sides of streams.

Although *Savery* invented some form of steam pump, steam power was first used on a large scale when *Newcomen* built a steam pump in about 1709:

NEWCOMEN'S STEAM PUMP

(*a*) Slow in operation.
(*b*) Fuel and power wasted by the need to inject cold water at each stroke.
(*c*) Costly in fuel.
(*d*) Needed constant attention in turning cocks on and off to admit jet of cold water.
(*e*) Inaccurate in construction.
(*f*) Could only pump, not turn machinery.

JAMES WATT (1736–1819)

He was an instrument maker who experimented on a model of Newcomen's engine and carried out *improvements*, producing his first engine in 1775:

(*a*) Separate condenser—cut out jet of cold water.
(*b*) Valve box—produced pressure above and below the piston.
(*c*) Air tight cylinder—aided by John Wilkinson.
(*d*) Rotary motion—aided by Murdock—enabled engine to drive machinery (1781).

He was assisted in his work by *Matthew Boulton* (1728–1809) who owned the Soho Works (Birmingham) and provided capital for the venture.

The first two engines were used at Bloomfield Colliery, Birmingham and by John Wilkinson at Brosley. In 1785–1786 the first rotary motion engines were supplied to a cotton mill in Nottinghamshire and the Albion Corn Mills, London. By 1800, 500 engines had been sold.

The application of steam power to factories resulted in:

(*a*) The expansion of factory system and the growth of the surrounding towns.
(*b*) Towns being situated near the source of steam power—the coalfields.

5. Coal

Coal, together with *iron* and the *steam engine*, was the *basis of the Industrial Revolution.*

SMALL DEMAND

In 1700 very little coal was mined because of its limited use:

(*a*) Domestic purposes.
(*b*) Brewing.
(*c*) Brickmaking.
(*d*) Some forges.

Poor communications hindered development. Only the Tyne Valley had a large production which was exported by sea to London.

INCREASED DEMAND AFTER 1750

Used for:

(*a*) Steam Engine

1709—Steam Pump—Newcomen.
1775—Steam Pump—Watt.
1781—Rotary Motion—Watt and Murdock.

(*b*) Application of Steam Engine to Transport

Railways:
1815—Locomotive 'Blucher'—George Stephenson.
1825—Stockton–Darlington Railway—'Locomotion No. 1'.
1829—'Rocket'—Stephenson.
1830—Liverpool–Manchester Railway.

Steamships:
1802—*Charlotte Dundas*—Symington.
1812—*Comet*—Bell.

(*c*) Increased domestic use due to improved transport.
(*d*) Use in the iron industry:

1709—Abraham Darby I smelted with coke.
1784—Puddling Furnace—Cort.

(*e*) Lighting by coal gas—invented by William Murdock about 1802.
(*f*) Increased exports (in millions of tons)—1791 exported ·3; 1850, 11.
(*g*) Development of electricity in late 19th century.
(*h*) Chemical products—tar (Dundonald), dyes (Perkins) and, later, synthetic textiles and rubber.
(*j*) Increase in population. In 1700 the population of Great Britain was 6½ million; in 1831 was 16 million.
(*k*) Technical improvements in mining (see below).

TECHNICAL IMPROVEMENTS IN MINING

Ventilation

c. 1730—Double shafts at Newcastle.
c. 1760—Brattices or doors to guide air.
c. 1790—Triple shaft and exhaust fan invented by Buddle.
1815—Safety lamps—Sir Humphry Davy and George Stephenson.

Drainage

1709—Newcomen's Steam Pump.
1775—Watt's Steam Pump.

Haulage Underground

c. 1600—Wooden rails.
c. 1750—Ponies (Newcastle).
1777—Cast-iron rails (John Carr).

Shafting and Hoisting

18th century—Cast-iron tubing to line shafts.
1839—Wire rope (Andrew Smith).
c. 1840—Metal cages wound by steam.

Surface Haulage

c. 1600—Wooden rails.
1738—Iron rails (Whitehaven).
1788—Flanged wheel (William Jessop).
1811—Steam locomotive with cogged wheel (Blenkinsop).
1815—Locomotive 'Blucher' (Stephenson).

Blasting

c. 1800—Gunpowder.
c. 1855—Compressed air coal cutters.
c. 1890—Electric coal cutters.

The coalfields with ironstone were the first to develop. As the 18th century advanced industry in general moved nearer the coalfields and this was even more the case in the 19th century.

6. Engineering

Before the Industrial Revolution the engineer did not exist. Accuracy was not essential and the skilled craftsmen did the job of making and repairing the simple machines of the time.

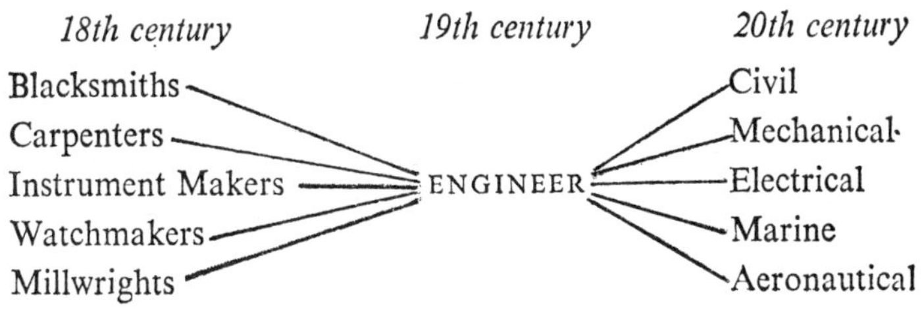

JAMES WATT

James Watt can be called the 'Father of the Engineers' because it was:

(*a*) his demand for accuracy, and
(*b*) his training of men to make accurate parts

that made engineering important.

MURDOCK

W. M. Murdock (1754–1839) trained with the firm of Boulton and Watt from 1777 and became foreman in charge of erecting steam engines. He developed his own ideas:

(*a*) In 1784 he designed a model locomotive but was discouraged by Watt.
(*b*) He helped Watt invent rotary motion (1781).
(*c*) Used coal gas as a means of lighting at the Soho Works, Birmingham (1802).
(*d*) Installed hot-water pipe heating at the baths of Leamington Spa.

RENNIE

J. Rennie (1761–1821) was also employed by Watt to help in redesigning factories and machinery to take the steam engine. On leaving Watt, he was responsible for a wide variety of projects:

(*a*) Kennet–Avon Canal.
(*b*) Rochdale–Lancaster Canal.
(*c*) Bridges—Waterloo, Southwark (iron), London (completed after his death).
(*d*) Docks—London, East India.
(*e*) Dockyards—Chatham, Sheerness.
(*f*) Harbours—Holyhead, Kingstown.

WILKINSON

J. Wilkinson (1728–1808) experimented at Bilston (Staffs) until he found a way of using coal for puddling and smelting iron. He also invented a boring machine for making cannons. This was used by Watt for making cylinders in his steam engine. He was known as 'Iron-Mad' Wilkinson, because of his enthusiasm for the use of iron in making such things as bridges, a boat, chairs, vats, pipes, his own coffin and gravestones out of iron.

BRAMAH

J. Bramah (1748–1814) trained Maudslay in his workshop and invented:

(*a*) Patent locks.
(*b*) Pull-over tap for public houses.
(*c*) The water closet.
(*d*) The hydraulic press, with Maudslay.

MAUDSLAY

H. Maudslay (1771–1831) set up his own workshop in 1797 and trained Roberts, Nasmyth, Clements and Whitworth. He invented:

(*a*) Screw-cutting lathe.
(*b*) A machine capable of measuring to the accuracy of one ten-thousandth of an inch.
(*c*) A slide rest.

ROBERTS

R. Roberts (1789–1864) invented:

(*a*) A self-acting mule based on Crompton's.

(*b*) A radial arm for winding in a metal plating machine.
(*c*) Other inventions connected with railways and steamships.

WHITWORTH

J. Whitworth (1803–1887) invented:

(*a*) A method of producing a really flat surface.
(*b*) A measuring machine for parts and tools.
(*c*) Standard sizes for screws and machine parts introduced by him leading to standardisation and mass production.

NASMYTH

J. Nasmyth (1808–1890) invented the steam hammer in 1839.

Out of all their workshops came a steady stream of mechanics and foremen who spread the skills and ideas learnt there.

The Second Industrial Revolution

After 1850 Great Britain was the Workshop of the World but lost pre-eminence as the century advanced.

The new industrial revolution was based on:

1. Steel.
2. Electricity.
3. Internal combustion engine.

1. Steel

1856—Bessemer invented Converter—but as it failed to remove phosphorus from steel could only use non-phosphoric ores.
1868—Open Hearth Process—again could only use non-phosphoric ores.
1878—Thomas-Gilchrist Process—allowed use of phosphoric ore by lining the furnace with materials absorbing phosphorus.

RESULTS

(*a*) Iron gradually replaced by stronger, more reliable steel.
(*b*) Extended use of steel in engineering, railway lines, building and armaments.

Britain's steel production increased but she was rapidly overtaken by the emergent nations of U.S.A. and Germany.

1901—Germany—6½ million tons.
G.B.—5 million tons.
U.S.A.—13½ million tons.

2. Electricity

1831—Michael Faraday invented the dynamo.
1884—Charles Parsons invented the turbine.

Britain lagged behind, despite invention of the above in this country, because:

(*a*) Less water power than in U.S.A.
(*b*) Vested interests in coal and steam strong.
(*c*) Gas still considered best for lighting, especially after invention of the gas mantle in the '80s.
(*d*) Difficult to obtain a private act of Parliament to start an electrical concern. Therefore, before 1914, Tyneside was the only place with electric power on a large scale.

3. Internal Combustion Engine

Again Britain lagged behind others (also see p. 37).

Need for Re-adjustment

(*a*) More adaptability to above inventions required.
(*b*) Economy vulnerable:
  (*i*) Overwhelming dependence on cotton export which was increasingly open to foreign competition.
  (*ii*) Increasing export of machinery to our overseas rivals.
  (*iii*) Compared with other nations, industry not sufficiently vigorous and elastic.

(*c*) *New industries:*
  (*i*) Road vehicles—especially after introduction of mass production in the '20s.
  (*ii*) Electricity—electrical apparatus manufactured more and more after creation of the National Grid in 1926. By 1935 90% of the population had electric power and factories had no need to be near a source of power.
  (*iii*) New skilled industries, *e.g.*, canning, chemicals, wireless apparatus, etc.

Mass production was on the increase and Britain's cotton industry and heavy industries based on coal declined in importance. However, with the energy crisis of the 1970s, the importance of coal as a source of energy to this country has grown with a need to revitalise the coal industry.

3

TRADE

Before Free Trade

Trade governed by the theory of MERCANTILISM in the early 18th century:

(*a*) Exports should exceed imports.
(*b*) Thus foreign gold would enter this country.
(*c*) Trade controlled to ensure this.

An expression of this may be seen in the Navigation Acts which helped protect British trade interests:

1651 Navigation Act

(*a*) All colonial goods should be carried in English or colonial ships.
(*b*) All European goods to be carried in English ships or ships of the exporting country.
(*c*) All coastal trade to be in English ships.
(*d*) All cargoes to be brought direct to England and not trans-shipped.

1660 Navigation Act

Similar to 1651 Act, but now, in addition, certain colonial goods (sugar, tobacco, cotton, indigo, ginger and dyewoods) had first to be exported to England and then re-exported. This was originally intended to harm Dutch trade, but it helped us to lose our American colonies, who were angered by the restrictions, and our trade would therefore have probably increased without these measures.

Growth of Free Trade

It originated in the work of *Adam Smith*, Professor of Economics at Glasgow University. In 1776 he wrote a book *Wealth of Nations* putting forward the theory of *laissez-faire*. When applied to trade it implied the abolition of duties on all imports and exports.

Early Influence

(*a*) Pitt codified customs regulations.
(*b*) Also concluded *Eden Treaty* (1786) with France:

(*i*) French wine to enter this country at the same rate of duty as Portuguese wines, *i.e.*, a preferential rate.
(*ii*) France reduced duties on English cottons, woollens, hardware and hosiery.

This treaty was cancelled because of the French Wars which started in 1793. The wars led to the Continental System.

1806—Continental System

Napoleon closed Continental ports to ships carrying British exports.

1815—Corn Laws

Free Trade further hampered at end of wars by the corn laws (for Anti-Corn Law League see p. 53).

Foreign corn could not enter this country until English corn was selling at 80*s*. a quarter.

Reforms

1. REFORMS OF HUSKISSON (President of the Board of Trade—1822–1828)

(*a*) Revision and easing of the Navigation Acts.
(*b*) 1828—introduced sliding scale to Corn Laws—the lower the price of English corn, the higher the duties on foreign corn.
(*c*) 1822–1828—reduced tariffs and internal taxes.
(*d*) Set an upper limit of 30% duty on imported goods.
(*e*) Repealed law forbidding emigration.
(*f*) Consolidated the existing tariff system.
(*g*) Wanted imperial preference.

2. REFORMS OF PEEL (1841–1846)

Continued reduction of tariffs:

(*a*) Raw materials to pay up to 5% duty.
(*b*) Partly manufactured goods up to 12%.
(*c*) Fully manufactured goods up to 20%.
(*d*) 1843—export of machinery freed.
(*e*) 1844—export and import duties on raw wool abolished.
(*f*) 1845—most raw materials admitted free.

(*g*) 1846—all raw materials admitted free and semi-manufactured goods, dairy produce, livestock and potatoes admitted free. Repeal of the Corn Laws (see p. 53).

3. REFORMS OF GLADSTONE (1853–1860)

(*a*) 1853—Duties reduced on 466 taxed articles.
(*b*) 1860—The 419 taxed articles reduced to 48—only 15 of importance left, including beverages, wine and timber. Customs duties intended for revenue only—not protecting British producers by keeping foreign goods out and therefore articles with high consumption rate taxed, *e.g.*, tea, sugar, beer, tobacco.
Income tax also used as a means to make up the deficit of revenue, *e.g.*, in 1860 raised from 9*d.* to 10*d.* in the pound.

Free Trade triumphant

Final measure was *Cobden's Commercial Treaty with France* (1860)—duties on French imports reduced. The loss on duties was offset by the increased trade which resulted.

For a few decades England and the rest of the world were in favour of Free Trade.

Return to Protection

Why?

(*a*) Growing industrialisation of other countries, especially America and Germany, after settlement of internal troubles.
(*b*) More protection in these new industrial countries to help the growth of their infant industries.
(*c*) Decline in British shipping and export of iron, coal and steel.
(*d*) Foreign countries, who had originally used British machinery, developed their own more modern methods and machinery.
(*e*) British manufacturers reluctant to use new methods, *e.g.*, use of electricity restricted by vested interests in steam.
(*f*) A growing movement to introduce Imperial Preference to give favourable rates of duty to the growing British Empire.
(*g*) In the period 1876 to 1885 Britain's share in world trade fell from 23% to 19%.

How?

1881—FAIR TRADE LEAGUE

Founded by Farrar Eckroyd—believed in Free Trade, but urged that Britain, in the circumstances, should use retaliatory duties to force other countries to reduce tariffs. Little sympathy in England; supported by some Conservatives, but not by the Party.

TARIFF REFORM CAMPAIGN

Launched by Joseph Chamberlain in 1903.

Aims

(*a*) Protection against foreign competition.
(*b*) Creation of Imperial customs union to make the Empire a single economic unit.

1906

Conservative Party defeated in the election on the issue of tariff reform.

1915—MCKENNA DUTIES

33% duty on clocks, watches and motor cars. Reason—to save war-time shipping space, but it was retained after the war was over.

1921—SAFEGUARDING OF INDUSTRIES ACT

Protected British industries by duties on various imports, mainly from Germany.

1931—BREAK WITH FREE TRADE

National Government adopted general tariff of 10% (later raised to 20%) because of the financial crisis.

1932—IMPORTS ADVISORY BOARD

To decide on measure of protection to be afforded to home industry.

Protection offered to British farmers by a price guarantee over and above the price of foreign corn.

1932—OTTAWA CONFERENCE

Duty placed on all foreign wheat, but not on dominion or colonial wheat.

Britain in the Early 20th Century

(*a*) By 1913 Britain was among equals rather than predominant.
(*b*) The idea of balancing agriculture and industry (*i.e.*, self-supporting) was abandoned.
(*c*) Depended on limited imports with a thriving export industry.

The 1914–1918 War

The economy adapted to suit conditions:

(*a*) Men taken from industry and agriculture into armed forces, but not conscripted in early years.
(*b*) Measures of centralisation and control of industry, *e.g.*, Munitions of War Acts (1915 and 1916).
(*c*) By 1918 the government controlled:

  (*i*) mines,
  (*ii*) all basic industries,

and regulated:

  (*i*) supply of all raw materials,
  (*ii*) distribution of finished products.

(*d*) In agriculture increased home production was required to counteract intensive submarine campaign. This was encouraged by:

  (*i*) guaranteed minimum prices,
  (*ii*) prohibition on raising of rents,
  (*iii*) wages boards—to set minimum wages for agricultural workers.

Britain emerged from the war victorious but she still faced all the old pre-war problems:

(*a*) Foreign competition.
(*b*) Higher tariff walls raised by rivals.
(*c*) Rivalry of other imperialist powers.
(*d*) Even greater dependence on imported food.

Depression Between the Wars

PATTERN

(*a*) A *mild boom* during which:

  (*i*) cotton and coal industries over-expand,
  (*ii*) iron and steel had excess capacity left over from the war,
  (*iii*) shipbuilding had surplus capacity.

(*b*) *Mid-1920*—rapid collapse, rising unemployment and general depression.
(*c*) *Winter 1921–1922*—unemployment reached 2 million.
(*d*) *Mid-1922 to mid-1924*—slow recovery of industry supplying home market, export trades depressed.
(*e*) *1924–1929*—world improvement but not in Britain—gradual fall in Britain's share of export trade.

(*f*) *World Slump* started with stock market collapse in U.S.A.—unemployed rose to 3 million—especially hit 'depressed areas', *e.g.*, Merthyr Tydfil and Jarrow had unemployment rate of 60% Led to:

(*i*) 1931—Abandonment of the Gold Standard—to help exports recover.

(*ii*) 1932—Protective Duties (see above).

(*g*) *End of 1930s*—depression lifted due to rearmament and then the Second World War.

CHARACTERISTICS OF DEPRESSION

(*a*) Mass unemployment—average rate of 22% at the height of the depression.

(*b*) A movement of population from North to South to the new light industries, *e.g.*, cars and electrical goods.

(*c*) Abandonment of Free Trade.

(*d*) More State intervention to improve social services for unemployed.

Since 1939–1945 War, Britain has been fighting a battle to balance her trade by means of increased exports and less imports. But this balance has yet to be achieved.

There have been three major problems:

(*a*) rising prices coupled with

(*b*) extensive wage claims,

(*c*) speculation on the £.

SOLUTIONS

(*a*) increasing the bank rate, e.g. up to 7% in 1961.

(*b*) limitations placed on capital expenditure (1957, 1961, 1968).

(*c*) credit restricted (1957, 1961, 1968),

(*d*) wages pause (1961) and wages freeze (1967) policies,

(*e*) setting up of government bodies to help control the economy—National Economic Development Council and Prices and Incomes Board.

The Common Market

1973—Britain enters Common Market, originally formed by France, West Germany, Italy and Benelux countries, despite fears of rising prices and a break with the Commonwealth especially over preferences. Britain's membership of the European Free Trade Association (EFTA) came to an end.

4

TRANSPORT AND COMMUNICATIONS

Roads

Very little was done about roads from the Roman times to the 18th century. They were a parish responsibility. The surveyor of highways (a man with no training) saw that each parishioner did his share of the work on the roads each year. This mainly consisted of filling in the larger holes in the road with stones.

18th-Century Traffic

1. PACK HORSES

Carried heavy goods and travelled in trains to a fixed timetable. Covered about 10 miles a day.

2. TWO-WHEELED CARTS

Carried merchandise mainly of a local nature.

3. FOUR-WHEELED WAGON

Carried poor passengers and long-distance heavy goods. Wide wheels and horses churned up the roads. Travelled about 10 miles a day.

4. STAGE COACH

Carried passengers and luggage. Reached speeds of up to 15 miles per hour.

5. MAIL COACH

Introduced by John Palmer of Bath in 1784, it carried mail and passengers. Reached up to 20 miles per hour at its fastest.

6. POST CHAISE

Lightest and fastest of all: the transport of the rich.

Turnpikes

First introduced during the reign of Charles II, but reached their heyday in the late 18th century. A Turnpike Trust of local gentry was organised and, by act of Parliament, was empowered to set up gates (turnpikes) where tolls could be collected; the money to be used for the upkeep of the roads.

Road building

This was a great period of road building. Three great road builders:

METCALF

Built many roads in the West Riding, although blind from early childhood.

TELFORD

Used a system of firm foundations and drainage in building numerous bridges and roads, *e.g.*, London to Holyhead.

MACADAM

Advocated a strong surface of uniform stones which would bind when traffic passed over them. He was made Surveyor-General of Roads for the whole of Britain.

Through the efforts of these men and the Turnpike Trusts, coach transport reached its peak, but it declined after 1830 due to increased competition from the railways.

Canals

Developed from waterways cut to shorten time taken to carry goods by river.

Difficulties of river transport

(*a*) Shallows and silt deposits.
(*b*) Meanders.
(*c*) Weirs.
(*d*) Water wheels.
(*e*) Fish traps.
(*f*) Narrowness of rivers.
(*g*) Low bridges and fords.

Canals built 1755–1777

1755—Canal alongside Sankey Brook (Warrington).

1761—Duke of Bridgewater's Canal designed to carry coal from duke's coalmines at Worsley to Manchester. This canal, designed by Brindley, cut the price of coal in Manchester by a half.

1773—Bridgewater Canal, again designed by Brindley, continued, so that it connected Manchester to Liverpool. It cut the cost and length of journey, *e.g.*, cotton carried at 6*s*. a ton instead of 40*s*.

1777—Grand Trunk Canal (Trent–Mersey) opened up Hull–Liverpool navigation and was also designed by Brindley.

The Canal Mania (1791–1794)

Canals were built all over the country, *e.g.*, Grand Junction Canal, Leeds–Liverpool Canal. In all, over 47,000 miles of canal were built. Some were never finished and never repaid shareholders, but they were of benefit to the growing industry of this country, especially for carrying heavy goods and raw materials. But in agricultural districts canals never repaid the cost of building. By the end of the 19th century half the canals were paying no dividend at all.

Decline of Canals

CAUSES

(*a*) Many canals were built by speculators to make money at the expense of the shareholders.
(*b*) The canal system was disjointed with no co-ordination between different localities. They failed to join together even with growing competition from the railways.
(*c*) No timetables, goods delayed on wharves (which led to pilfering) and lack of through rates for long distances.
(*d*) Barges using power found canals too narrow and speed damaged the banks.
(*e*) Numerous locks hindered navigation—about one every mile.
(*f*) The canals were unsuitable for the carriage of mail and passengers.
(*g*) The railway companies interfered by buying up parts of canals and closing them thus blocking through routes.

ATTEMPT TO STOP DECLINE

1845—Canal Carriers Act was passed:

(*a*) It allowed canal companies to run their own barges.
(*b*) Allowed companies to vary tolls and lease them to other canal companies to make through rates easier.

Some canals are still in use today, many have fallen into decay and they are no longer the lifelines of industry that they were in the 18th century.

Railways

Twin origin:

(*a*) Locomotives.
(*b*) Railroads at collieries.

Evolution of the Locomotive

(*a*) Carts pulled by various methods:

(*i*) Manpower.
(*ii*) Horses.
(*iii*) Gravity.
(*iv*) Sails.

(*b*) Steam locomotives developed at the collieries because:

(*i*) The patent on Watt's steam engine expired in 1800.
(*ii*) The development of accurate machine tools led to higher steam pressure and lighter engines.
(*iii*) The growing expense of horses, especially during the Napoleonic Wars.

As engines developed at the collieries one main name became predominant:

GEORGE STEPHENSON

He was brought up at a Northumberland colliery, where his father was a fireman on a stationary steam engine. He was self-taught, working in collieries driving a gin horse and rising to be a fireman.

1814—Designed and used a locomotive, 'Blucher', successfully on the tramroads of Killingworth Colliery.

1825—Completed the Stockton–Darlington Railway using 'Locomotion No. 1' and horse-drawn carts, mainly for the carriage of coal.

1830—Completed the Liverpool–Manchester Railway which was the first passenger railway using the locomotive 'Rocket' which had won the Rainhill Trials in 1829.

This marked the beginning of the 'Railway Mania' which lasted into the 1840s during which railways were built without due regard to their economic necessity.

Early Railways

OPPONENTS OF THE EARLY RAILWAYS

(*a*) *Vested interests* in other forms of transport—coaches, coach-builders, horse breeders, innkeepers and canal owners.

(*b*) *Landowners* thought that railways:

(*i*) Would ruin productivity.
(*ii*) Would reduce value of their land.
(*iii*) They thought that the price of their land would rise if they held on to it.

(*c*) *Certain towns and newspapers*, usually connected with vested interests or landowners.
(*d*) *Sabbatarianism.*

REASONS FOR HIGH COST OF EARLY RAILWAYS

(*a*) High price of land.
(*b*) Many lines built by trial and error and much money wasted.
(*c*) Many lines duplicated.
(*d*) No standard equipment.
(*e*) Individual acts of Parliament, surveyors, lawyers, etc., required for each line, and this was expensive.
(*f*) The topography of Great Britain demanded expensive cuttings, bridges, etc.
(*g*) Engineers had to build solidly and safely to encourage the public to use the railways.
(*h*) Much bribery needed to buy off other interests.

BENEFITS GRANTED BY RAILWAYS

(*a*) Factories able to move away from source of raw materials because raw material could now be more easily obtained and distributed by rail.
(*b*) Because Great Britain was the first to develop railways she had an advantage over her industrial rivals.
(*c*) Iron and coalfields developed away from waterways.
(*d*) Iron and steel industry expanded because of increased orders from railways.
(*e*) Cost of living reduced because goods became cheaper with quick, easy transport.
(*f*) Stock piles at factories could be smaller, as they could be replenished easily, and thus there was less deterioration.
(*g*) Firms were able to expand on a nation-wide basis.
(*h*) Labour was transported more easily from place to place.
(*j*) Agriculture improved—animals and perishables travelled more quickly.
(*k*) Deep-water trawling encouraged by growing markets due to quick transport.
(*l*) Dormitory suburbs grew.
(*m*) People took holidays away from home and therefore health improved and holiday resorts grew.
(*n*) Decline in regional differences.

MOTIVES FOR BUILDING RAILWAYS

(*a*) Other transport congested, slow, unreliable and costly.

(*b*) Commercial and industrial expansion.
(*c*) Fear that rival towns and cities would take the lead.
(*d*) Large profits to be made.
(*e*) Enormous amount of capital made available by inventions.
(*f*) Strategy—railways used to gain power by means of amalgamation, *e.g.*, George Hudson, the Railway King.

DISCOMFORTS OF EARLY RAILWAY TRAVEL

(*a*) Open carriages for poorer classes.
(*b*) Sometimes lack of third-class carriages.
(*c*) Unreliability of some of the early steam locomotives.
(*d*) Lack of co-ordination between different railway companies over timetables, fares, etc.
(*e*) No adequate signalling system.
(*f*) No fog signalling system.
(*g*) Train crews often untrained.
(*h*) Lack of refreshment and restaurant cars.
(*j*) No toilet facilities.
(*k*) Early carriages makeshift and uncomfortable.
(*l*) Inadequate braking systems.

Parliament's Attitude to Railways

(*a*) Welcomed railways as competition for canals.
(*b*) Allowed acts of Parliament to incorporate companies to run lines.
(*c*) Hoped lines would compete with each other—frustrated to a certain extent by George Hudson.
(*d*) Reluctant to interfere in the running of railways—*laissez-faire* attitude.

Eventually Parliament had to do something about the chaotic situation which developed.

1839—Turnpike principle abandoned and railways now carried the mail.
1842—Inspectors appointed who could postpone the opening of lines, obtain traffic returns and investigate accidents.
1844—Railway Act—companies had to run return trains on their lines each day with a third-class fare of 1*d.* a mile.
1849—Establishment of the *Railway Clearing House:*

(*a*) Enabled through bookings to be made.
(*b*) Co-ordinated timetables.
(*c*) Allowed railway companies to use each other's lines.
(*d*) Enabled sharing of profits to take place.

Improvements

(*a*) Padded third-class seats.
(*b*) Adequate signalling system.
(*c*) Steel rails replaced iron.
(*d*) Restaurant cars introduced.
(*e*) Sleeping cars brought into use.
(*f*) Better braking system used.

1871—All accidents had to be notified by companies and an enquiry had to be made by the Board of Trade.
1873—Railway Commission established.
1888—Commission made permanent and authorised to fix fare rates and goods rates.

Amalgamation

Started with such early pioneers as George Hudson. The government ignored it until 1853, when it forbade the fusion of the Midland Railway and the London North Western Railway. But it carried on, *e.g.*, the Great Western Railway took over four smaller companies to carry the line on to Penzance. Before 1914 there were about half a dozen companies.

1914–1920—State control during the war period.
1923—Amalgamation into four great companies—L.N.E.R., L.M.S., G.W.R. and S.R.
1939–1945—State control during the war—companies paid a lump sum per year and State retained receipts.
1947—*Nationalisation* by Transport Act:

(*a*) Transport Commission to control railways.
(*b*) Transport Tribunal to approve fares and goods rates.

Shipping

Ships originally built of wood. Later came wood and iron and the first iron boats appeared on canals in 1787.

Advantages of Iron Hulls

(*a*) Lighter because of trimmer sides.
(*b*) Stronger and easier to repair.
(*c*) Longer hulls possible.
(*d*) Cheaper to make.

(*e*) More cargo space available because less room taken up by supports.
(*f*) Sharper hulls and bows and therefore ships move faster.
(*g*) More watertight.
(*h*) Less danger of fire.

New improvements led to development of shipping lines which carried mail and kept to fixed timetables:

1835—*Great Western* sailed Atlantic in thirteen days.
1840—Cunard began a regular mail service to America.

Originally *paddle steamers* were used but they had their *defects:*

(*a*) Rolling—one paddle in and one paddle out in heavy seas.
(*b*) As the large amount of coal required was consumed *en route* the draught of the ship varied creating navigational difficulties.
(*c*) Wind and water resistance increased.
(*d*) Could not manage a fast turn and therefore did not get full use of engines.

Sail versus Steam

Competition between sail and steam grew after:

(*a*) Introduction of screw—not affected by rolling and had more power.
(*b*) Tubular boilers—compact and gave more power.
(*c*) Compound engine (1860)—economised in fuel.
(*d*) Opening of Suez Canal (1869) shortened the routes to the Far East.
(*e*) Introduction of steel hulls—new ships too large to take sails.
(*f*) Invention of steam turbine.

Safety at Sea

(*a*) 1800–1830—Trinity House built lighthouses.
(*b*) 1836—Trinity House to build all lighthouses.
(*c*) 1824—Establishment of the National Lifeboat Institution.
(*d*) 1850—Board of Trade made responsible for Merchant Navy.
(*e*) 1875–1876—Merchant Shipping Acts:

(*i*) Owners could be penalised for unseaworthy ships.
(*ii*) Limit put on deck cargoes.
(*iii*) Plimsoll load line established.

Postal Services

Mail carried by horseback and, from 1784, by the mail coach.

1830—Post carried by the Liverpool–Manchester Railway.
1838—First travelling Post Office on the Birmingham–Liverpool line, in a converted horse box—later special post-coaches designed. Money orders introduced.
1840—Penny post, the work of Rowland Hill (1795–1879), later Secretary of the Post Office. Before this letters charged by distance and weight, *e.g.*, a single letter sheet from London to Manchester cost 10*d.*
1855—Pillar boxes first erected in London.
1861—Post Office Savings Banks.
1870—Post cards and halfpenny stamps introduced.
1881—Postal orders first issued.
1911—Mail first carried by air (Hendon to Windsor).
1919—Regular air mail from London to Paris.

The diversity of postal services has increased over the years, *e.g.*, special rates for printed papers, recorded delivery, etc., but the postal service loses money today largely due to the increased use of the telephone.

Telegraph

First practical use of electricity was to send messages.

1836—Cooke and Wheatstone's Electric Telegraph—needles tilted to indicate different letters.
1840—Wheatstone produced ABC Needle Telegraph, an improvement on the above.
1845—Morse Code brought into use—a series of dot and dash sounds sent by wire and invented by an American, Samuel Morse (1791–1872).
1851—First submarine cable between Dover and Calais.
1866—First successful Atlantic cable laid by the *Great Eastern*.
1869—Telegraphy in Great Britain taken over by the Post Office.
1876—The telephone invented by Alexander Graham Bell (1847–1922), a Scotsman living in Canada.
1889—The National Telephone Company formed from the amalgamation of many private companies that existed previously.
1891—First submarine telephone cable (London–Paris).
1892—Trunk lines taken over by the Post Office.

1912—Post Office took over all telephone undertakings except the service run by Hull Corporation which is still the only privately owned service.
1927—Trans-Atlantic telephone service inaugurated.
1929—The Post Office adopted the teleprinter (invented by F. G. Creed) in which an electronic typewriter sends a telegraph message to another typewriter.

There has been a steady increase in the number of telephone subscribers in this country using such inventions as the public call box, the automatic (dial) telephone and, lately, the car telephone. This is the one Post Office service which regularly makes a profit.

Wireless

1896—After experiments by his own company and the Post Office, Marconi sent wireless messages over short distances.
1901—First trans-Atlantic wireless message sent by Marconi.
1907—Post Office expanded interests to twelve radio stations—cheap radiotelegrams became available.
1922—Broadcasting began in Britain with the B.B.C. at Savoy Hill.
1927—Post Office took control of wireless telephony, the first service being between London and New York. Later other countries came into the system, *e.g.*, Australia in 1924.
1936—B.B.C. opened first television at Alexandra Palace. Television invented by James Logie Baird in 1926.
1955—The Independent Television Authority put out its first television programmes.
1967—Colour television introduced on BBC 2 network.

Modern Travel

Linked with two developments:

1. Electricity.
2. Internal Combustion engine.

Electricity

(*a*) In 1831 Michael Faraday put forward the principle of the *dynamo*.
(*b*) In 1884 Sir Charles Parsons produced the *turbine*, a powerful engine motivated by steam or water which could generate electricity.

Resulted in:

(*i*) Electrified tramways, *e.g.*, Leeds 1891.
(*ii*) London Underground electrified in early 20th century.

Internal Combustion Engine

1876—Otto invented silent gas engine.
1895—Dr Rudolph Diesel invented the engine named after him.

In the 1880s Gottlieb Daimler was using a small light-oiled engine in a car. Resulted in:

(*a*) 1881—Daimler operated first car on the road.
(*b*) 1895—First motor exhibition in London.
(*c*) 1896—The 'Red Flag' Act of 1865, which had restricted speed of cars to 4 m.p.h. in towns, was repealed. After this the supremacy of the railways was challenged, but motor transport only became the more important form of transport after 1914–1918 War.
(*d*) 1904—London General Omnibus Company obtained first licence for mechanical traction and introduced a standardised petrol bus in 1910.
(*e*) Steady increase in the number of cars on roads especially with standardisation and mass production introduced by William Morris in the 1920s in England and Henry Ford in America, until now the roads are choked with traffic especially in towns.

AIR TRAVEL

1905—Wright Brothers stayed in the air for half an hour covering 24½ miles.
1909—Bleriot crossed the Channel by air.
1919—Passengers first carried by air—initially limited to a cross-Channel service.
1920—Parliament gave power to cities to build airports.
1930—Bristol opened first public airport, followed by Manchester and Glasgow.
1939–1945—Two major inventions to assist in the development of air travel were the jet engine and radar.
1946—British Overseas Airways Corporation and British European Airways set up by Labour Government. Regular Atlantic air services inaugurated.

The 50s and 60s have seen the growth in the size of passenger jet aircraft which is leading to the 'jumbo' jet, e.g. Anglo-French Concorde of the 1970s.

5

POPULATION AND HEALTH

Population

Slow Growth up to 1750

In part due to low birth rate but mainly due to HIGH DEATH RATE. This was caused by:

(*a*) The low standard of living.
(*b*) Lack of vitamins causing such diseases as scurvy and rickets.
(*c*) Lack of food if the harvest was bad—the staple food was bread, making for little variety—sometimes a little salted meat, peas or cheese might supplement this.
(*d*) Lack of medical knowledge—doctors could describe diseases but could rarely cure them—poor could not afford medical help which was, in any case, usually inadequate and insanitary.
(*e*) Overcrowding—houses built hurriedly, especially in towns.
(*f*) Lice and other vermin which carried disease.
(*g*) No adequate sanitation.
(*h*) Polluted wells leading to diseases spread by water.
(*j*) Lack of easily washable clothing—mostly made from wool.
(*k*) Widespread infections:

plague
typhus
typhoid
smallpox
cholera.

Population Changes 1750–1831

1. Population in 1750 was 8 million, in 1831 was 16 million.
2. By 1831:
   (*a*) More people were town dwellers.
   (*b*) Towns had grown in size.
   (*c*) More people were living in the North and in the mining areas.
3. In 1700 there were only seven towns with a population of over 20,000. By 1831 there were seven with a population of over 100,000: London, Liverpool, Glasgow, Manchester, Leeds, Edinburgh, Birmingham.

4. The pattern of employment was changing. More people were working in industry, less in agriculture, but the occupations, in order of importance, were:

    Agriculture
    Domestic workers, Building workers, Cotton-mill operatives, Coal miners — still far behind agriculture, in numbers employed

Reasons for Population Increase after 1850

(*a*) The *Industrial Revolution* led to a greater export of manufactured goods and thus, in exchange, this country was able to import a wider variety of foodstuffs and a better diet resulted.

(*b*) The *Death Rate fell* whilst the *Birth Rate rose:*

(*i*) Improved midwifery halved the infant death rate by the mid-19th century.

(*ii*) Better water supplies became available. Water came through pipes instead of being drawn from insanitary wells, pools or rivers.

(*iii*) Local councils given more power, by Acts of Parliament, to improve drainage, lighting, paving and to clear slums.

(*iv*) Cheaper and more easily washable cotton clothing.

(*v*) Medical improvements—inoculation against smallpox (Jenner), antiseptics (Lister and Pasteur), anaesthetics (Simpson) and an improved professional nursing service (Florence Nightingale), all led to improved conditions in medical treatment and in hospitals.

Public Health

Problems

1. HOUSING

Closely packed housing on a back-to-back or court system, poorly constructed and lacking essential services such as water supply and drainage. Also a window tax on small houses until 1825 and on large houses until 1851, which resulted in many people bricking-in windows to avoid the tax.

2. REFUSE

Allowed to accumulate in the streets until there was enough to make it worthwhile to collect. Sewers only intended for rainwater.

3. WATER

Wells near cess-pools and cemeteries. Sometimes water drawn from polluted rivers. If from standpipe only turned on infrequently.

4. OPEN SPACES

Not many open spaces as there was a prejudice against fresh air. It was not felt to be beneficial.

5. ALCOHOL

Excessive drinking caused bad health—drink cheap and no licensing hours.

6. MALNUTRITION

Lack of vitamins and correct type of food—not enough money to buy correct food, and ignorance of dietetics.

7. HOSPITALS

Too few, voluntary and inadequate. Poor only had Poor Law doctors.

8. LACK OF LOCAL AUTHORITIES

Few corporations existed before 1835. Where they did exist they were often ineffectual and corrupt.

9. WORKING CONDITIONS

Long hours, low wages and low standard of living produced apathy.

10. LAISSEZ-FAIRE

A general hostility to government intervention and an exaggerated respect of private property was prevalent.

Public Health Legislation

1835—MUNICIPAL CORPORATIONS ACT

(*a*) Councils to be elected by ratepayers.
(*b*) Accounts to be audited and published.
(*c*) Corporations *could* pave, light and cleanse streets (*i.e.*, they now had the power to do these things but were not legally bound to).

Because of (*a*) and (*b*) corporations became less corrupt and more likely to promote good health among citizens.

1838—TYPHUS EPIDEMIC IN LONDON

(*a*) Bad health put a burden on the poor rate.
(*b*) Poor Law Board to investigate health of towns. Reported in *1840*—recommended better building, sewage disposal and setting up of local boards of health.

1848—PUBLIC HEALTH ACT

(*a*) Central Board of Health set up in London.
(*b*) Local Boards of Health set up.
(*c*) Local Boards *could* appoint surveyors and medical officers, *could* cleanse, pave, light streets, provide clean water, parks and drainage.

Central Board could not compel local boards to do anything.

1853

Powers of Central Board taken over by a board of ministers.

1858–1869

Little interest in public health—no great cholera epidemics.

1869

Public Health Commission reported:

(*a*) Conditions just as bad.
(*b*) Sanitary laws should be made UNIFORM, UNIVERSAL and IMPERATIVE.

1871

Local Government Board appointed to look after health and the poor.

1872—PUBLIC HEALTH ACT

Divided the country into urban and rural sanitary districts.

1875—PUBLIC HEALTH ACT

Authorities:

(*a*) Had to have medical officers and sanitary inspectors.
(*b*) Had to supply water and build sewers.
(*c*) Had to provide protection against infectious diseases.
(*d*) Had to deal with 'nuisances'.
(*e*) Could seize and destroy unsound food.
(*f*) Had to make, pave, clean and light the streets.

1868—ARTISANS AND LABOURERS DWELLINGS ACT

Local Authorities could condemn unfit property and if repairs were not carried out could demolish it.

1919

Councils to build houses for rent.

Ministry of Health set up.

After the war of 1939–1945 the problem of housing was magnified by extensive bombing and it has been the task of every government since then to try to provide adequate accommodation for all.

6

POOR LAW

Early Efforts

1601—Elizabethan Poor Law

Each parish responsible for its own poor. Overseer of the Poor collected poor rate from each landowner. He also:

(*a*) Apprenticed pauper children.
(*b*) Gave the aged and infirm money, food, etc., or provided them with a home.
(*c*) Gave work or money to the able-bodied, who could not find other employment.
(*d*) Sent people able, but refusing, to work to prison.

1662—SETTLEMENT ACT

Settlers who came to a parish and could not give an assurance that they would have work within forty days were forced to leave by the Overseer of the Poor.

These provisions broke down because:

(*a*) The overseers became lax.
(*b*) The Industrial Revolution led to the growth of new towns not covered by the Poor Law.
(*c*) Farm labourers flooded towns and fell on poor rate, because taxes and prices rose, common land disappeared and land lost due to enclosures.

1795—Speenhamland System

Came about because of breakdown in the Elizabethan Poor Law system.

The magistrates of Speenhamland (Berks.) met to decide on fixing wages but instead devised a scheme of fixing a scale of relief based on:

(*a*) A man's wages.
(*b*) Whether married.
(*c*) Number of children.
(*d*) Price of bread.

For this they drew up a Bread Scale incorporating these conditions.
Certain major difficulties arose:

(*a*) Allowances became a subsidy to wages and masters tended to lower wages accordingly.
(*b*) Hard work unrewarded and saving penalised.
(*c*) Improvident marriages encouraged.
(*d*) Farms abandoned where the poor rate levied was heavy.
(*e*) Poor relief came to be regarded as a right, and therefore more people applied for it.
(*f*) Much corruption and extravagance.

Workhouse System

1782—GILBERTS ACT

Unions of parishes COULD build workhouses, if they wished, and pool the costs involved.

1832—POOR LAW COMMISSION

To investigate the system existing at the time which had become out of date during the Industrial Revolution.
Their recommendations led to:

1834—POOR LAW AMENDMENT ACT

(*a*) Parishes to form unions of parishes to build workhouses.
(*b*) Workhouses to be harsh and strict to discourage people from entering them (known as the less eligible principle).
(*c*) Workhouses to be segregated.
(*d*) Unions to be controlled by Boards of Guardians elected by ratepayers.
(*e*) A Poor Law Commission set up in London to control the system.

Criticism

(*a*) The Commission, with Edwin Chadwick as secretary, was excessively harsh and noted for economy, legality and efficiency.

(*b*) No central control of the Boards of Guardians who were financially independent.

(*c*) Bitter opposition in the North of England and Guardians refused to make the act work.

(*d*) Workhouses became mixed.

In 1847 the *Poor Law Commission* became the *Poor Law Board* responsible to Parliament and in 1871 became part of the Local Government Board.

Modern System

Development

No investigation until early 20th century.

1905—POOR LAW COMMISSION

(*a*) Reported 14,000 children in workhouses.
(*b*) Lunatics mixed freely with other inmates.
(*c*) 200,000 to 300,000 children receiving outdoor relief.
(*d*) 30% of the poor were sick or infirm.
(*e*) Relief being given to the aged, sick, infirm and mothers with children—not the original intention of the act, which was primarily to help the able-bodied poor.
(*f*) There had been no enquiry since 1834 and the system had become mechanical.
(*g*) Sick receiving inadequate relief—Poor Law doctors overworked and lunatics sometimes employed as nurses.

There was disagreement over what should be done about the problem:

Majority Report—replace Poor Law by a Public Assistance Committee to be helped by Voluntary Aid Committees.

Minority Report—system to be broken up gradually:

(*a*) Poor to be responsibility of local councils.
(*b*) Children of school age to be under Education Committee.
(*c*) Infirm, aged and children under school age to be under Health Committee.
(*d*) Lunatics to be under care of Asylum Committee.

1908—OLD AGE PENSIONS ACT

A non-contributory pension of 5*s*. a week to all persons over the age of seventy—7*s*. 6*d*. for married couples.

1909—LABOUR EXCHANGE ACT

Set up by the efforts of Winston Churchill. Offices in most large towns and cities where employees could enquire about prospects of work and employers could advertise their wants.

1911—UNEMPLOYMENT INSURANCE ACT

(*a*) Covered unemployment insurance and health insurance.

(*b*) Contributions by employers and employees.
(*c*) Subsidy from the State.
(*d*) Included most manual and many non-manual workers.

1918—MACLEAN COMMITTEE

They could not reconcile the two reports of the 1905 Commission, and no action was taken until 1929.

1929—LOCAL GOVERNMENT ACT

Boards of Guardians abolished, and transferred their poor law functions to county councils and county boroughs.

1930—POOR LAW ACT

(*a*) Only aged and infirm to be in workhouses.
(*b*) Outdoor relief to be given if necessary.
(*c*) Local councils to look after orphans.

1935—POOR LAW ACT

Able-bodied poor to come under Unemployment Board.

1942—BEVERIDGE REPORT

Reports of the Beveridge Commission that was set up during the Second World War. They recommended that:

(*a*) Want should be prevented rather than cured.
(*b*) A national insurance scheme should be established which covered more risks and offered more benefits than previously.

1945

(June)—Family Allowances—5*s*. per child after the first.
(July)—Labour Party returned to power.

1946—CURTISS REPORT

Findings:

(*a*) Lunatics still in the workhouses and sick still mixed with other inmates, spreading disease.
(*b*) Workhouses dirty.
(*c*) Staffs overworked.

1946—NATIONAL HEALTH SERVICE

A comprehensive, free, medical, dental and welfare system set up.

1948—NATIONAL ASSISTANCE ACT

(*a*) Relief under government control.

(*b*) National Assistance Board set up.
(*c*) The board to assist blind persons, tubercular cases, the aged and vagrants.

By the mid-'50s the Board was having to grant a large amount of direct monetary aid which had not been envisaged in the original act.

1964

Second post-war Labour Government increased the scope of assistance:

(*a*) redundancy payments,
(*b*) increased family allowances,
(*c*) increased benefits for pensioners and widows,
(*d*) free school meals for the fourth child in a family and above. (Since withdrawn.)

7

FACTORY ACTS

1802–1832

Conditions of labour were poor in the 18th century:

(*a*) No public regulation of factory buildings—badly lit, insanitary, ill-ventilated, dangerous machinery unguarded leading to accidents.
(*b*) Cheap 'slave' labour—women and children especially pauper 'apprentices' from the age of three upwards.
(*c*) Long hours—up to sixteen a day.
(*d*) Employees had no bargaining power with employers.

Early Abortive Acts

1802—HEALTH AND MORALS OF APPRENTICES ACT

Due to the work of Sir Robert Peel Senior, a Tory mill-owner. It only applied to apprentice (workhouse) children:

(*a*) Twelve hours work per day.
(*b*) No night work.
(*c*) Had to receive instruction in the 3 Rs.
(*d*) Church and Sunday School compulsory.
(*e*) Regulations on ventilation and cleanliness.

Disadvantages

(*a*) 'Free' children replaced the workhouse children—not covered by Act.
(*b*) Factory inspectors were magistrates who were often mill-owners themselves and therefore not impartial.

1819—COTTON FACTORY ACT

Due to the efforts of Robert Owen, a mill-owner from New Lanark, Scotland:

(*a*) No child under nine to work.
(*b*) Children (9–16 years) to work 12 hours.

Failure because:

(*a*) Only applied to cotton mills.

(*b*) Inspection left to local magistrates.
(*c*) No proof of ages—no registration of births till 1836.

'THE TEN-HOUR MOVEMENT'

This movement was led, first of all by Oastler and Sadler and later by Lord Shaftesbury. They attempted to get the 10-hour day in the textile factories, mainly for women and children, but in the hope that it would automatically apply to men as well.

1831

Ten-Hour Bill introduced, but shelved.

1832

Shaftesbury takes over leadership of the movement in Parliament.

1833–1853

1833—FACTORY ACT

(*a*) Applied to ALL textile mills.
(*b*) Children (9–12 years) to work 9 hours per day.
(*c*) Young persons (13–18 years) to work 12 hours per day.
(*d*) Each child to have 2 hours schooling per day.
(*e*) Four independent factory inspectors appointed.

Defects

(*a*) Not enough inspectors.
(*b*) No satisfactory proof of age.
(*c*) Many factories had no public clock.
(*d*) Children still worked in relays, therefore men still had to work very long hours.

Shaftesbury was successful in the passing of:

1842—MINES ACT

(*a*) Employment in mines of women and boys under ten forbidden.
(*b*) Mines' inspectors appointed.

1844—FACTORY ACT

(*a*) Women to be treated on same basis as young persons (13–18 years).
(*b*) Machinery to be in operation between 5.30 a.m. and 8.30 p.m.
(*c*) Factories to have public clocks.
(*d*) Children to spend half time in school.
(*e*) Dangerous machinery to be guarded.

This act only applied to textile mills.

1846

Ten-Hour Bill rejected.

1847—FACTORY ACT

Women and young persons to work 12 hours (allowing 2 hours out of the 12 for meals), but shifts still possible as long as machinery could be working between 5.30 a.m. and 8.30 p.m. and so men did not get the 10-hour day.

1850—FACTORY ACT

(*a*) Women and young persons to work 10½ hours per day.
(*b*) Machinery to operate between 6 a.m. and 6 p.m. but children (9–12) could still work in shifts until the 1853 Act.

1853—FACTORY ACT

Children to carry out their work between 6 a.m. and 6 p.m., with 1½ hours for meals. So, in effect, the 10-hour day for men was achieved as they could not work without the aid of the children, but this *only* applied in textile mills.

Extension of the Factory Acts (1853–1877)

1863–1867—CHILDREN'S EMPLOYMENT COMMISSION

Reported on bad conditions in pottery, matches and lace-making industries.

1867—FACTORY ACTS EXTENSION ACT

Factory laws extended to cover further industries, *e.g.*, iron and engineering and all industries employing more than fifty people in one place.

1867—WORKSHOP REGULATION ACT

(*a*) Workshop defined as a place, other than a factory, in which children, young persons and women employed in handicraft.
(*b*) Children under eight not to be employed.
(*c*) Half-time for those between eight and thirteen.
(*d*) Twelve-hour day for women and young persons—beginning to be brought into line with the legislation already affecting the textile mills.
(*e*) Local authorities to be inspectors.

Defects

(*a*) Too many exceptions to the definition of an 'establishment over fifty workers'.

(*b*) Application left to the local authorities.
(*c*) Relay system still possible.
(*d*) Did not apply to men-only establishments.

1870—EDUCATION ACT

Allowed School Boards to enforce school attendance up to age of thirteen. (1876—school attendance up to thirteen compulsory.)

1871—FACTORY AND WORKSHOPS ACT

Workshops to be inspected by factory inspectors.

1874—FACTORY ACT

(*a*) Women and young persons—10-hour day (as in textile industry).
(*b*) Minimum working age nine (and a year later—ten).
(*c*) Half-time work for children up to fourteen.

1878—FACTORY AND WORKSHOPS ACT

(*a*) Factories re-defined as an establishment using mechanical power.
(*b*) Existing acts improved and consolidated.

Thus the factory acts were extended to all industries although establishments employing men only were still not regulated.

Further Factory Acts

1880—EMPLOYERS' LIABILITY ACT

Employers liable for negligence of their workers.

1888–1890

Reports of a *Select Committee* of the House of Lords on the 'sweated trades', *e.g.*, tailoring, bootmaking, cutlery, etc.

1891—FACTORY AND WORKSHOPS ACT

(*a*) Minimum working age eleven.
(*b*) Dangerous trades designated.
(*c*) More safety rules.

1895—FACTORY ACT

(*a*) Children under thirteen to have 30-hour week.
(*b*) No night work for under fourteens.

(*c*) Docks, wharves, quays and laundries brought under factory acts.
(*d*) Home Secretary to make rules about places where only men employed.

1897—WORKMEN'S COMPENSATION ACT

Employer responsible for accidents in some dangerous trades.

1901

Minimum working age twelve.

1906—WORKMEN'S COMPENSATION ACT

Employers liable for all accidents in all trades.

1918—EDUCATION ACT

Half-time system abolished.

1937—FACTORY ACT

(*a*) Women and young persons (16–18 years)—48-hour week.
(*b*) Young people under 16—44-hour week.
(*c*) More stringent regulations on lighting, temperature, sanitation, etc.
(*d*) New establishments to be covered by acts, *e.g.*, film establishments.

1938—YOUNG PERSONS' EMPLOYMENT ACT

The hours of certain other young persons outside factories, *e.g.*, errand boys and messengers, were brought into line with those covered by the 1937 Act.

1944—EDUCATION ACT

School-leaving age raised to fifteen and later to be sixteen. When this part of the act is enforced in 1970, no one below the age of sixteen may be employed in a factory.

1948—FACTORIES ACT

(*a*) Extended 1937–1938 acts.
(*b*) Medical supervision of young persons in factories.
(*c*) Seats to be provided at work not only for breaks but for work, if convenient.
(*d*) Inspection of certain equipment, *e.g.*, ropes and chains.

8

WORKING-CLASS MOVEMENTS

Anti-Corn Law League

Founded in 1839. *Leaders*—Cobden and Bright.

Aims

Abolition of the Corn Laws (see pp. 22, 23).

Aids

(*a*) Penny Post—able to send out literature and notices cheaply.
(*b*) Railways—speakers able to travel up and down the country.

Main Arguments

(*a*) 'Dear Loaf'—Corn Laws were putting up the price of bread—won support of the working classes.
(*b*) Foreign countries paid for manufactured goods with corn therefore the Corn Laws restricted foreign trade—won support of the middle classes.

Progress

Great at first but popularity depended on the price of corn. Peel, Prime Minister at the time, was in favour of repeal but feared the reaction of his party.

A solution to the problem was forced on him by two events in *1845:*

(*a*) A bad harvest.
(*b*) The potato famine in Ireland.

This led to the repeal of the Corn Laws in *1846*, which resulted in a split in the Tory Party and Peel losing his post as Prime Minister.

Chartism (1837–1848)

A movement which presented a petition, called the *Charter*, to Parliament containing millions of signatures.

Leaders

Lovett and Place—wished to work peacefully through Parliament.
Feargus O'Connor—in favour of physical force.

Reasons for Movement

Disappointment with:

(*a*) 1832 Reform Bill.
(*b*) Poor Law Amendment Act 1834.
(*c*) Failure of the Grand National Consolidated Trade Union.

Aims

(*a*) Reform of Parliament and method of voting.
(*b*) Reform of the Poor Law.
(*c*) Better education.
(*d*) Free press.
(*e*) Factory regulations.
(*f*) Repeal of the Corn Laws.
(*g*) Temperance reforms.
(*h*) Smallholdings for workers.

Methods

(*a*) Petition (2–3 million signatures, but many false) sent to Parliament. This charter demanded:

(*i*) universal manhood suffrage.
(*ii*) secret ballot.
(*iii*) annual parliaments.
(*iv*) equal electoral districts.
(*v*) payment of M.P.s.
(*vi*) abolition of the property qualification for M.P.s.

(*b*) Held Chartist's Congress.
(*c*) Sacred Month—general strike.
(*d*) Riots.

Why it failed

(*a*) Parliament and ruling classes united strongly against them.
(*b*) Firm government repression.
(*c*) Disunity over aims and methods, especially between the leaders.
(*d*) Lack of discipline.
(*e*) Lack of funds.
(*f*) Other movements more popular, *e.g.*, Anti-Corn Law League offered more immediate benefits.
(*g*) Lack of good communications.

Friendly Societies

Origin

Members joined together to pay into a central fund from which they obtained insurance against sickness and unemployment. These benefits had been included in the social functions of the mediaeval guilds.

17th and 18th Centuries

(*a*) Small local societies set up known as *village* societies, usually connected with public houses. Held annual gatherings in the form of a feast or a walk, *e.g.*, Bottesford Society of 1747.
(*b*) In towns they began to move onto a national basis—some were open to one trade only, *e.g.*, London Sailmakers' Burial Club, but most open to people of different trades.

1793—ROSE'S ACT

(*a*) Societies given recognition in law.
(*b*) Any number of persons given the right to form a society of good fellowship to raise premiums to supply mutual benefits.

After 1799 Combination Acts (see p. 57) many trade unions carried on under the guise of friendly societies.

By 1800 several thousand societies existed in this country, *e.g.*, the Royal Order of Shepherds.

19th Century

Rapid growth in numbers and large centralised institutions grew up, *e.g.*, Independent Order of Odd Fellows.

Often in *difficulties* in early days because it was hard to calculate risks as they lacked the knowledge, and thus they often paid out too much money and had to close down.

ACTS OF PARLIAMENT

1829—All registered societies to keep a proper check on sickness and mortality rates thus enabling standard tables to be drawn up to determine premiums.
1846—Friendly Societies' Act—all rules to be deposited with a Registrar of Friendly Societies, a civil servant.
1896—(*a*) All societies to register with the Registrar.
(*b*) Exemption from income tax on their funds.

20th Century

1911—National Insurance Act used friendly societies to pay out sick benefits—discontinued after National Insurance Act of 1946.

1955—Friendly Societies Act authorised societies to invest surplus funds in other registered societies.

By 1961—had invested funds of about £191 million and had 4¼ million members.

Co-operative Movement

An attempt to eliminate the element of competition in trading to the mutual benefit of members of the co-operative society.

Robert Owen attempted this with his co-operative communities and his co-operative shop at New Lanark. But although these experiments failed, his ideas and writings were very influential among socialists.

1844 Rochdale Pioneers

FORMATION

By flannel weavers in Toad Lane, Rochdale, on the principles of Robert Owen.

AIMS

(*a*) To distribute profit amongst members as dividend on purchases.
(*b*) Goods of high quality to be sold—an effort to counteract the poor, and often adulterated, goods sold in the 'truck' shops.
(*c*) To educate the workers.
(*d*) To allow each member to vote on the affairs of the company.

RESULTS

(*a*) Stopped sale of bad food.
(*b*) Encouraged saving.
(*c*) Educated workers.
(*d*) Gave workers business experience.
(*e*) Rapid extension of the co-operative societies.

LANDMARKS

1846—Classed as a friendly society.
1862—Became a limited liability company.
1864—Formation of the Co-operative Wholesale Society:

(*a*) Made purchases on a larger scale than individual societies.
(*b*) Produced goods of its own.

1869—Co-operative Congress first held—co-ordinates work of the societies and meets annually.

The co-operative movement offered support to the Labour Party through its own political party and by the formal alliance of this party with the Labour Party.

Trade Unionism

Early Trade Clubs

Formed by skilled workers. By paying small subscriptions they were able to pay out sick pay, death benefits and unemployment pay. They met in inns and did not use strike action but sent petitions to King or Parliament.

Opposed by rich employers who persuaded Parliament that:

(*a*) The machinery, which trade clubs opposed was making England a rich country.
(*b*) Revolution would spread from union activity.
(*c*) If J.P.s fixed wages, as demanded by the clubs, export trade would be ruined.

Led to:

1799—*Combination Acts*—forbade forming of unions of workmen against masters and masters against men.

This was not enforced against masters as Parliament was not afraid of their power growing, and their influence was strong.

1814 onwards—Place attempted to obtain the repeal of the Combination Acts.

1824—Repeal of the Combination Acts.

Grand National Consolidated Trade Union

Formed by Robert Owen, Socialist factory owner, in 1834—a federation of trade unions.

AIMS

(*a*) To obtain, with the advantage of size, better bargaining power with the employers.
(*b*) To transform the union, sooner or later, into a producers' co-operative.
(*c*) To stage a peaceful general strike leading to a peaceful revolution.

FAILED WITHIN A YEAR:

(*a*) Energy expended in dispersed wage negotiations.
(*b*) Example made of six Dorchester farm labourers (Tolpuddle

Martyrs) sentenced to seven years' transportation to Australia for taking illegal oaths (*i.e.*, oaths of allegiance to unions).

(*c*) The 'Document'—employers forced workers to sign a document before they employed them saying that they were not members of a trade union.

(*d*) Working class lacked education, stability and experience.

New Model Trade Unions

LEADERS

Applegarth, Newton and Allen.

They wished to work within the capitalist system, to avoid striking and use of force.

ORGANISATION

(*a*) National organisation of skilled men of the same craft.

(*b*) Members paid high subscriptions.

(*c*) Friendly society benefits paid.

(*d*) Organised T.U. committees in each major town and city.

LANDMARKS

1868—First *Trade Union Congress* in Manchester.

1867—*Hornby* v. *Close* case. (Test of the legality of T.U.s.) Boilermakers' Union prosecuted Treasurer of the Bradford branch for stealing £24. Because the T.U.s were in restraint of trade they were illegal and the court could do nothing.

This led to:

1868—*Royal Commission on Trade Unionism.*

Applegarth and Allen organised evidence and witnesses.

This was followed by:

1871—*Trade Union Act*

(*a*) A trade union was a legal organisation even if in restraint of trade.

(*b*) Their funds were to be protected by trustees.

1871—*Criminal Law Amendment Act*

Strike action declared illegal.

This weakened the power of the unions by depriving them of one of their main weapons.

1875—*Conspiracy and Protection of Property Act*

(*a*) Picketing legalised.
(*b*) No action by a trade union to be treated as criminal if the same action could be done legally by an individual.

New Unionism

SIGNIFICANCE

(*a*) *Socialist Ideas* spread by:

(*i*) Hyndman who knew Karl Marx—tried to popularise his theories, *i.e.*, the destruction of private property and replacement by communal ownership. In 1881 he founded the Democratic Federation (later the Social Democratic Federation) to spread Marxist ideas. He wrote the book *England for All.*
(*ii*) Henry George—wrote *Progress and Poverty*. The Great Depression of the 1880s encouraged the spread of Socialist ideas.

(*b*) Trade Unions spread to *unskilled and black-coated workers.*
(*c*) *Strike Action* increased:

1888—Bryant and May matchgirls staged a successful strike for a pay rise.
1889—Gasworkers' and General Workers' Union got an 8-hour day after the threat of a strike.
1889—Great Dock Strike—the dockers demanded a fixed wage of 6*d.* per hour and went on strike when their demand was refused. They obtained the rate mainly due to the mediation of Cardinal Manning.

SIGNIFICANCE OF SUCCESS

(*a*) Unions charging small subscriptions spread.
(*b*) New Unions pushed out Model Trade Unions in the Trade Union Congress.
(*c*) New Unions start to secure legislation through Parliament and help to secure representation in Parliament for T.U.s.

The Labour Party

FORMATION

1888—The Scottish Labour Party was formed by Kier-Hardie with a mainly Liberal policy plus nationalisation of the railways and the banks.
1892—Three Labour M.P.s (Kier-Hardie, Havelock–Wilson and

Burns) in Parliament supported by the trade unions, the Social Democratic Federation and the Fabian Society.

1895—Bradford Conference—the T.U.s, S.D.F., the Fabian Society and the Scottish Labour Party form the Independent Labour Party (I.L.P.).

AIMS

State control and ownership of the means of production and distribution.

PROGRAMME

(*a*) Eight-hour day.
(*b*) Sick benefits.
(*c*) Unemployment benefits.
(*d*) Widows' pensions.
(*e*) Help for the infirm.

DEVELOPMENT

This programme was not accepted by some because they thought it was too Communist. So in

1899—The T.U.C., Co-operative Movement, S.D.F. and the Fabian Society founded the Labour Representative Committee (secretary—Ramsay MacDonald).
1900—Two candidates elected as M.P.s out of fifteen nominations.
1906—Twenty-nine M.P.s elected—encouraged by Liberal social reforms.
1918—Sixty M.P.s elected—became the official opposition.
1924—First Labour government.
1929—Second Labour government—later to become a Coalition under Ramsay MacDonald.
1945—First Labour government with an overall majority, under Clement Attlee.

Trade Unions and the Law

1901–1913

1901—Taff Vale Strike

After this strike, the Amalgamated Society of Railway Servants were sued by the Taff Vale Railway Company for taking strike action. The case was taken to the House of Lords and the Union lost and had to pay £23,000 damages.

Trade unions had thought that they were protected by the 1871 and 1875 Acts, but this case proved the contrary (see pp. 58, 59).

1906—Trades Dispute Act

Trade union funds could not be touched in law as compensation for strikes.

1908—Osborne case

Osborne, a member of the Amalgamated Society of Railway Servants, sued the union for using union funds for political purposes. He won his case, which was a great blow to many Labour M.P.s, who were supported by union funds.

1911

Payment of Members of Parliament, eased the situation a little.

1913—Trade Union Act

(*a*) T.U. was now legally allowed to use funds for politics if the majority of the members agreed.
(*b*) Payments for political purposes were to be kept in a separate fund.
(*c*) Members could withdraw from the political fund if they wished.

TRADE UNIONS FROM 1913–1927

1913

Revival of Robert Owen's ideas of bigger, concentrated unions and large-scale strikes.

1914

Miners, railwaymen and transport workers formed the *Triple Alliance.*

1921

Miners' Strike failed when they received little support from other members of the Triple Alliance. The alliance collapsed.

1926—General Strike

In support of the miners, the T.U.C. called out all members. It lasted nine days and then collapsed.

Led to

1927—Trade Union Act

(*a*) General and sympathetic strikes illegal.
(*b*) State employees not to belong to unions with political ties.

This weakened the trade unions:

(*a*) 1920—membership was 8 million.
(*b*) 1932—membership was 4½ million.

TRADE UNIONS FROM 1927

Growth in strength:

1945—membership was 7·8 million.
1962—membership was 9·8 million.

1946—Repeal of 1927 Trade Union Act.
1963—*Rookes v Barnard* case ruled that strikers could be prosecuted for acts of intimidation against workers unwilling to strike.
1965—Trade Dispute Act—reversed the *Rookes v Barnard* judgement.

9

EDUCATION

Early 19th Century

Education for the Poorer classes

1. PROFIT MAKING

There was a fee of 3*d.* to 9*d.* per week.

(*a*) Common day school—no inspection of teachers, buildings or equipment and no standards of teaching and cleanliness.
(*b*) Dame schools (infants)—teachers unfit for other work—rooms dirty, overcrowded and unhealthy.

2. PRIVATE SUBSCRIPTION SCHOOLS

Mainly run by two church societies:

(*a*) British and Foreign Schools Society (Nonconformist).
(*b*) National Society for the Education of the Poor in the Principles of the Established Church (Church of England).

Taught the 3 Rs, geography and general knowledge. Fees not more than 1*d.* per week. Run on the MONITORIAL SYSTEM—the teacher taught selected pupils who taught the lesson to other pupils.

Merits of the Monitorial System

(*a*) Cheap—only one teacher needed.
(*b*) Good training for monitors.
(*c*) Stimulus to other pupils because they wished to become monitors also.

Criticisms

(*a*) Lack of discipline with monitors in charge.
(*b*) System mechanical and parrot-like.

3. CHARITY AND SUNDAY SCHOOLS

(*a*) To combat popery.
(*b*) To keep the poor in their place.

Charity schools—in workhouses and factories—taught reading, writing and the catechism with, perhaps, a trade.

Sunday schools—aimed at stamping out hooliganism on Sunday and providing education for children working throughout the week—mainly teaching from the Bible.

Education for the richer classes

(*a*) Governess.
(*b*) Private school or tutor.

Government Intervention

1833

Whig government granted £20,000 for building schools; 50% of the cost to be raised by the particular organisation involved and the rest of the cost of the building granted from the fund. Mostly administered by the church societies. One defect was that the richer areas tended to get more money.

Attitudes to Education

There was still strong opposition to education of the poor:

(*a*) Churches—wanted State aid but no State control.
(*b*) Certain Whigs were afraid that the cost of education would mean higher taxation and that the Tories would use the schools for propaganda purposes.

Some were in favour of education.

(*a*) Utilitarians—wanted education for all on a purely secular basis.
(*b*) Radicals—favoured provision of money for schools of all denominations.

1839—Education Commission

Recommended:

(*a*) Increase in the grant to £30,000—passed by Parliament.
(*b*) Money to be distributed on the advice of inspectors—passed by Parliament.
(*c*) Setting up of teacher training colleges—not passed.

1846—Pupil-teacher system introduced

(*a*) Prospective teachers apprenticed to a headmaster for five years.
(*b*) Could then proceed to a training school for one, two or three years.

Increase in grant

(*a*) In 1847 to £100,000.
(*b*) In 1850 to £125,000 and in same year inspectorate increased to 21.

1858—Newcastle Commission

'To consider the extension of sound and cheap education to all classes'. They discovered that:

(*a*) One child in eight was at school.
(*b*) Of these a quarter were at private schools receiving poor education.
(*c*) Of the remainder, 80% left before the age of twelve.
(*d*) Half the children attended for less than 100 days.
(*e*) Teaching inefficient.
(*f*) Only moderate standard reached—children could spell simple words, make bills, write letters. They knew the position of countries and had a knowledge of the scriptures.

PROPOSALS

(*a*) Costs of education to come from the rates—not passed.
(*b*) Grants to be paid on the basis of results; 'payment by results'—passed in 1861.

This was more economical and grants fell by £176,000, but this system led to much parrot-like learning in order to qualify for a grant.

1870—Forster's Education Act

(*a*) School districts set up.
(*b*) Each district to have adequate school accommodation for its population.
(*c*) Existing schools to be used, but if insufficient, a School Board was elected.
(*d*) School Boards COULD build new schools and COULD compel attendance.
(*e*) Board Schools to exclude denominational religious instruction.
(*f*) Board Schools to be aided from rates and taxes.
(*g*) Voluntary schools could still receive money from the State if they introduced the 'timetable conscience clause', *i.e.*, religion to be taught at the beginning or end of the school session.
(*h*) Grants could be used for any purpose.

CRITICISMS

(*a*) No free education, although fees were refunded in necessitous cases.
(*b*) No compulsion.
(*c*) Voluntary schools received no rate aid.
(*d*) Churches disapproved—lack of religious instruction.
(*e*) National system of education not established.
(*f*) 'Payment by results' retained.
(*g*) No minimum number of attendances by each child required.

1876—Sandon's Act

(*a*) School attendance compulsory between five and thirteen.
(*b*) Children under ten not to be employed—employer to be fined £2 if he did so.
(*c*) Children between ten and thirteen could be employed if they were proficient in the 3 Rs.
(*d*) Children employable if they had a certificate proving they had attended school for a certain period.

1880—Mundella's Act

Compulsory attendance for children up to the age of thirteen.

1886

(*a*) Five million children on the registers.
(*b*) Three and a half million attended regularly.
(*c*) Thousands never attended.

1888—Cross Commission

Found that:

(*a*) There were good school facilities but many absentees.
(*b*) Money not producing right results.
(*c*) Still remnants of the monitorial system.
(*d*) Still only 3 Rs taught with needlework for girls.
(*e*) Optional subjects—singing, English, geography and science. The upper forms might do mathematics, chemistry, physics, Latin and French.

1902—Balfour's Act

(*a*) School Boards abolished.
(*b*) County boroughs and county councils to run schools.
(*c*) Actual work to be carried out by Education Committees consisting of councillors and co-opted members.

(*d*) Rate aid for voluntary schools.
(*e*) Voluntary schools had to have 'timetable conscience clause', with regard to religious instruction. Other subjects to be under the control of the local authority.
(*f*) Education authorities to provide facilities for training teachers.
(*g*) Education authorities to aid in the growth of higher education.

1918—Education Act

(*a*) Fixed the ages of five to fourteen as those for compulsory attendance.
(*b*) Gave local authorities further powers to improve the provision of schools in their areas.

Further Action 1926–1941

HADOW REPORTS (1926 and 1930)

Break between junior and senior education to be made at eleven plus.

1936—EDUCATION ACT

School-leaving age to be raised to fifteen. To be enforced from September 1st 1939 but prevented by the outbreak of war.

1938—SPENS REPORT

Reported on the organisation and integration of schools catering for children beyond the age of eleven.

1941—NORWOOD COMMITTEE

Suggested changes in the secondary school curriculum and studied the question of school examinations.

1944—Education Act

(*a*) Fees in state secondary schools abolished.
(*b*) Elementary education revised:

  (*i*) Primary education—infant and junior.
  (*ii*) Secondary education—modern, grammar and technical.

(*c*) School-leaving age to be fifteen and, later, sixteen.
(*d*) Advocated the setting up of county colleges with either full-time or part-time students.
(*e*) Grants for higher education to be increased.

1959—Crowther Commission

Advised:

(*a*) An early raising of the school-leaving age to sixteen.
(*b*) The speedy erection of some county colleges.

1965

The Labour Government decided upon a speedy move to Comprehensive Education and required all local authorities to submit plans.

Emancipation of Women

Despite increased elementary education of women and the extension of votes to all male ratepayers (Reform Acts of 1867 and 1884), women did not have the vote in the early 20th century. In higher education Oxford did not allow women to receive degrees until 1919.

Suffragettes

A militant movement aiming at obtaining votes for women and the right for them to sit in Parliament; at its height in the years prior to the 1914–18 War.

LEADERS

Mrs Pankhurst and her daughters Christabel and Sylvia.

METHODS

(*a*) Marches and militant meetings.
(*b*) Chaining to public buildings.
(*c*) Hunger strikes when in jail.

SUCCESS

Came after the First World War in which women worked in factories, agriculture and some military organisations, and showed their ability in these spheres.

1918—All women over thirty granted the vote.
1928—All women over twenty-one given the vote.
1919—Lady Astor the first woman M.P. to take her seat.
1924—Margaret Bondfield first woman member of the government.